COMPARING ANIMAL TRAITS

RUBY-THROATED HUMMINGBIRDS

TINY HOVERING BIRDS

REBECCA E. HIRSCH

Lerner Publications ◆ Minneapolis

Lerner Publications Company
A division of Lerner Publishing Group, Inc.
241 First Avenue North
Minneapolis, MN 55401 USA

For reading levels and more information, look up this title at www.lernerbooks.com.

Photo Acknowledgments

The images in this book are used with the permission of: © iStockphoto.com/SteveByland, pp. 1, 6, 18; © iStockphoto.com/CarolinaBirdman, pp. 4, 7, 13, 24; © iStockphoto.com/epantha, p. 5; © Phil Seu Photography/Getty Images, p. 8; © Education Images/UIG/Getty Images, p. 9 (left); © Pat Gaines/Moment/ Getty Images, p. 9 (right); © Jeff R Clow/Moment/Getty Images, p. 10 (left); © Michelle Chaplow/Alamy, p. 10 (right); © Nature Picture Library/Alamy, p. 11 (top); © Photoshot Holdings Ltd/Alamy, p. 11 (bottom); © Laura Westlund/Independent Picture Service, p. 12; © George Grall/Getty Images, p. 14; © Alan Murphy/ BIA Minden Pictures/Getty Images, p. 15; © RGB Ventures/Superstock/Alamy, p. 16; © Danita Delimont/ Gallo Images/Getty Images, p. 17 (left); © LOOK Dei Bildagentur der FotografenGmbH/Alamy, p. 17 (right); © DansPhotoArt/Getty Images, p. 19; © Charles Melton/Visuals Unlimited/Getty Images, p. 20; © William Leaman/Alamy, pp. 22, 29 (left); © blickwinkel/Alamy, p. 23 (top); © Cyril Ruoso/Minden Pictures/Getty Images, p. 23 (bottom); © Donald A Higgs/Getty Images, p. 25; © Terry Wall/Alamy, p. 26; © Arco Images GmbH/Alamy, p. 27; © Gerald de Hoog/Minden Pictures/Getty Images, p. 28; © Astrid Kant/Minden Pictures /Getty Images, p. 29 (right).

Front cover: © Larry Keller/Moment Open/Getty Images.
Back cover: © Steve Byland/Shutterstock.com.

Main body text set in Calvert MT Std 12/18. Typeface provided by Monotype Typography.

Library of Congress Cataloging-in-Publication Data

Hirsch, Rebecca E.
    Ruby-throated hummingbirds : tiny hovering birds / by Rebecca E. Hirsch.
        pages cm. — (Comparing animal traits)
    Includes bibliographical references and index.
    Audience: Ages 7 to 10.
    Audience: Grades 4 to 6.
    ISBN 978-1-4677-9508-1 (lb : alk. paper) — ISBN 978-1-4677-9631-6 (pb : alk. paper) —
ISBN 978-1-4677-9632-3 (eb pdf)
    1. Ruby-throated hummingbird—Juvenile literature. I. Title.
    QL696.A558H57 2015
    598.7'64—dc23

2015015213

Manufactured in the United States of America
1 – BP – 12/31/15

TABLE OF CONTENTS

MEET THE RUBY-THROATED HUMMINGBIRD

In a backyard garden, a ruby-throated hummingbird sips nectar from a flower. Then, *zip*! The hummingbird disappears in a blur. Ruby-throated hummingbirds are a kind of bird. Other kinds of animals you may know are insects, fish, amphibians, reptiles, and mammals.

An adult male hummingbird hovers in midair. Male ruby-throated hummingbirds are more colorful than females.

Birds share certain traits. All birds are vertebrates, animals with backbones. They are warm-blooded, meaning they keep their body temperature steady and make their own heat. They have feathers and beaks, and they lay hard-shelled eggs.

Ruby-throated hummingbirds share these traits. In some ways, ruby-throated hummingbirds are similar to other birds. But these colorful birds have some traits that make them unique.

CHAPTER 1

WHAT DO RUBY-THROATED HUMMINGBIRDS LOOK LIKE?

Ruby-throated hummingbirds are tiny, colorful birds. They are only 3 to 3.5 inches (7.6 to 9 centimeters) long, about the length of an adult's thumb. They weigh about 0.1 ounces (3.1 grams), less than the weight of a nickel.

The shiny feathers of the ruby-throated hummingbird seem to change color in different lights.

Ruby-throated hummingbirds have bright green feathers on their heads and backs and whitish-gray feathers on their undersides. Males have a patch of red feathers on their throats, and females do not. Sometimes the male's throat patch looks black. When the light strikes at the right angle, the feathers look bright red.

Ruby-throated hummingbirds have short wings that beat very fast. They have long, thin beaks and long tongues. These help the birds sip nectar from deep within tube-shaped flowers. Ruby-throated hummingbirds are good fliers, but they have tiny legs and cannot walk. They can only hop a little or scoot sideways on a tree branch.

DID YOU KNOW?
Ruby-throated hummingbirds are big eaters. An adult eats its weight in nectar **EVERY DAY**.

RUBY-THROATED HUMMINGBIRDS VS. ANNA'S HUMMINGBIRDS

An Anna's hummingbird hovers in midair as it drinks nectar from a flower. Anna's hummingbirds live along the Pacific coast of North America. These tiny birds are 3.5 to 4 inches (9 to 10 cm) long, slightly bigger than ruby-throated hummingbirds. An Anna's hummingbird weighs a bit more than a ruby-throated hummingbird too. These birds weigh about 0.15 ounces (4.3 g).

Both Anna's hummingbirds and ruby-throated hummingbirds have shimmering feathers. Both have green feathers on their heads and backs and pale feathers on their undersides. Male Anna's hummingbirds have a rose-pink patch on their throats, similar to the male ruby-throated hummingbird's bright red throat.

Both Anna's hummingbirds and ruby-throated hummingbirds have long, thin bills for sipping nectar from flowers. Both birds have short, powerful wings. Like ruby-throated hummingbirds, Anna's hummingbirds can beat their wings very fast.

COMPARE IT!

RUBY-THROATED HUMMINGBIRDS

VS.

ANNA'S HUMMINGBIRDS

**UP TO
3.5 INCHES
(9 CM)**

 ◀ LENGTH ▶

**UP TO
4 INCHES
(10 CM)**

Metallic green on back,
whitish-gray underside

◀ COLOR ▶

Metallic green on back,
pale gray underside

**LONG AND THIN FOR
SIPPING NECTAR**

 ◀ BEAK ▶

**LONG AND THIN FOR
SIPPING NECTAR**

RUBY-THROATED HUMMINGBIRDS VS. AUSTRALIAN PELICANS

An Australian pelican swims across a sunny lake. It tips forward and dips its head into the water, searching for fish. Australian pelicans are one of the largest flying birds in the world. These waterbirds are much bigger than ruby-throated hummingbirds. Australian pelicans can be 5.5 feet (1.7 meters) long and weigh more than 15 pounds (6.8 kilograms).

Australian pelicans and ruby-throated hummingbirds don't look much alike. Ruby-throated hummingbirds have brightly colored feathers. Australian pelicans have white bodies and black wings. Ruby-throated hummingbirds have tiny legs. Australian pelicans have strong legs and duck-like feet for swimming.

The ruby-throated hummingbird (*left*) looks very different from the Australian pelican.

An Australian pelican holds a fish in its bill.

Ruby-throated hummingbirds have long, thin beaks. An Australian pelican has a large bill with a pouch underneath. The pelican eats by scooping water and fish into its pouch. It drains the water, throws back its head, and gulps down the fish.

DID YOU KNOW?
The Australian pelican has the longest beak of any bird. It can be up to **20 INCHES** (51 cm) long.

CHAPTER 2

WHERE DO RUBY-THROATED HUMMINGBIRDS LIVE?

During summer, ruby-throated hummingbirds breed **across eastern North America.** They live in woodlands, meadows, forest edges, and along streams. They also live in backyards, parks, and gardens.

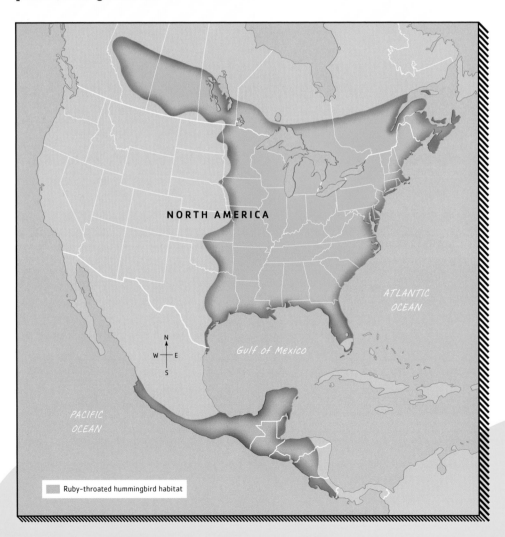

NORTH AMERICA

ATLANTIC OCEAN

Gulf of Mexico

PACIFIC OCEAN

Ruby-throated hummingbird habitat

Ruby-throated hummingbirds migrate when flowers and insects become scarce in winter. They spend winter in Mexico and Central America. They prepare for migration by eating a lot and storing fat. They use the stored energy to fuel their trip.

In both summer and winter habitats, ruby-throated hummingbirds eat a range of foods. They are omnivores. Ruby-throated hummingbirds sometimes catch flying insects and pluck spiders from webs. Mostly, they feed on nectar. As they go from flower to flower, they spread tiny grains called pollen. This helps the plants make seeds and reproduce.

Ruby-throated hummingbirds nest in trees. They weave nests the size of walnuts using spider silk, thistle, cattail, or bits of dandelion. They camouflage the outside of their nests with tiny pieces of lichen and moss.

DID YOU KNOW?
Many ruby-throated hummingbirds fly **500 MILES** (805 kilometers) across the Gulf of Mexico during their migration. The nonstop flight takes almost an entire day and night.

RUBY-THROATED HUMMINGBIRDS VS. ORCHARD ORIOLES

An orchard oriole perches high in a tree. It plucks red berries with its long, pointy beak. Orchard orioles live and breed in eastern North America. Like ruby-throated hummingbirds, orchard orioles live in many different habitats.

Orchard orioles live in woodlands and marshes, at the edges of forests, and on the shores of rivers and lakes. Like hummingbirds, orchard orioles need trees in their habitat for nesting. They weave their nests from grasses and line the nests with bits of plants, grass, and feathers.

The female orchard oriole is green and yellow, and the male is brown and black.

Orchard orioles are omnivores. They pick insects and spiders off leaves to eat. They also eat berries and other fruits and drink nectar from flowers. Orchard orioles migrate in fall when food becomes scarce. They fly long distances and spend the winter in South America.

RUBY-THROATED HUMMINGBIRDS VS. ADÉLIE PENGUINS

Adélie penguins waddle across a rocky coast. One by one, they dive into the icy sea. The habitat of an Adélie penguin is very different from the habitat of the ruby-throated hummingbird.

Ruby-throated hummingbirds live in woods, meadows, backyards, parks, and gardens. Adélie penguins live in Antarctica. In summer, they breed and raise their young on rocky coasts and small islands. In winter, they live on large chunks of ice at sea.

Hummingbirds fly through their habitat. Adélie penguins don't fly. They swim. They waddle to the water's edge and dive in. Hummingbirds are omnivores, and Adélie penguins are carnivores. They eat fish, squid, and small shrimplike creatures called krill.

COMPARE IT!

RUBY-THROATED HUMMINGBIRDS

VS.

ADÉLIE PENGUINS

EASTERN NORTH AMERICA, MEXICO, AND CENTRAL AMERICA ◄ RANGE ► **ANTARCTICA**

Woodlands, meadows, forest edges, shores of streams, parks, gardens, and backyards ◄ HABITAT ► Rocky coasts, islands, and oceans

NECTAR, INSECTS, AND SPIDERS ◄ DIET ► **FISH, SQUID, AND KRILL**

17

CHAPTER 3

RUBY-THROATED HUMMINGBIRDS IN ACTION

Along a bubbling stream, a ruby-throated hummingbird darts from flower to flower. It stops in midair at a spiderweb and plucks a spider to eat. Then the speedy bird zooms away.

Ruby-throated hummingbirds are fast fliers. By beating their wings forty to eighty times per second, they can fly up, down, forward, backward, and even upside down. They can stop instantly and hover in midair. This fancy flying allows them to sip nectar from flowers, catch flying insects, and pick spiders from spiderwebs.

DID YOU KNOW?

A hummingbird's wings beat so fast that they make a **HUMMING** sound, which is what gives the hummingbird its name.

Ruby-throated hummingbirds are able to catch flying insects.

When not feeding, a ruby-throated hummingbird perches on a twig. It keeps watch, looking from side to side. If a male hummingbird spots another hummingbird in his territory, he chases the bird away. If the other bird doesn't leave, the male ruby-throated hummingbird attacks with his beak and feet.

RUBY-THROATED HUMMINGBIRDS VS. RUFOUS HUMMINGBIRDS

A rufous hummingbird zips through a backyard. The hummingbird's wings are a blur. Rufous hummingbirds live in forests, meadows, parks, and gardens in western and southern North America. Ruby-throated hummingbirds and rufous hummingbirds behave in similar ways.

Both ruby-throated hummingbirds and rufous hummingbirds are acrobatic fliers. Rufous hummingbirds beat their wings fifty-two to sixty-two times per second. They can fly in all directions, stop instantly, and hover. With these moves, they can sip nectar from deep inside flowers and pluck insects from the air.

Like ruby-throated hummingbirds, rufous hummingbirds drink nectar from flowers.

COMPARE IT!

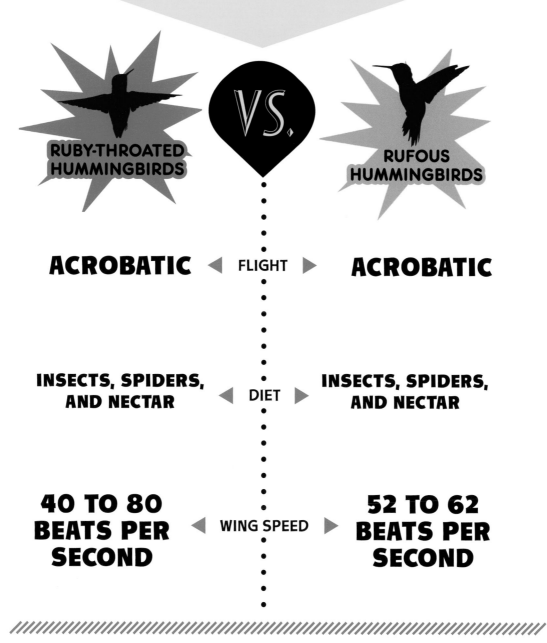

RUBY-THROATED HUMMINGBIRDS VS. **RUFOUS HUMMINGBIRDS**

ACROBATIC	◄ FLIGHT ►	**ACROBATIC**
INSECTS, SPIDERS, AND NECTAR	◄ DIET ►	**INSECTS, SPIDERS, AND NECTAR**
40 TO 80 BEATS PER SECOND	◄ WING SPEED ►	**52 TO 62 BEATS PER SECOND**

Like ruby-throated hummingbirds, rufous hummingbirds are fighters. They chase and battle other hummingbirds that visit their flowers and food sources. Rufous hummingbirds are such good fighters that they chase and attack much larger birds.

RUBY-THROATED HUMMINGBIRDS VS. TURKEY VULTURES

Turkey vultures soar in wide circles over a forest. They are looking for carrion to eat. Turkey vultures are black birds with bald, red heads. They live in farmlands, fields, and forests across North America and South America. These birds behave quite differently than ruby-throated hummingbirds.

Ruby-throated hummingbirds fly on quickly beating wings. A turkey vulture barely flaps its wings. It holds them outstretched in a V-shape and makes wide, wobbly circles in the sky. As the turkey vulture soars, it uses its keen eyes and strong sense of smell to find food on the ground.

Turkey vultures can soar for hours. A group of soaring turkey vultures is called a kettle.

Turkey vultures feed on carrion. Unlike hummingbirds, turkey vultures eat together. They gather in groups at the body of a dead animal. One or two vultures rip off meat with their hooked beaks. The others wait nearby for their turn.

A group of turkey vultures feasts on carrion.

CHAPTER 4

THE LIFE CYCLE OF RUBY-THROATED HUMMINGBIRDS

Male ruby-throated hummingbirds fight and chase other males from their territories. If a female enters a male's territory, he tries to get her to mate. He quickly dives around her and shows his red throat feathers.

After mating, the female builds a nest and lays one to three white eggs the size of peas. She incubates the eggs for two weeks, until the young hummingbirds hatch. Ruby-throated hummingbird chicks are tiny, bare of feathers, and helpless. The female raises the young on her own.

Two male ruby-throated hummingbirds fight in midair.

The mother hummingbird brings the chicks small insects and spiders to eat. In about three weeks, the chicks are ready to live on their own. After one year, the young hummingbirds are mature and ready to find mates. A female raises up to three broods, or groups of young, in a year. Ruby-throated hummingbirds live for three to nine years.

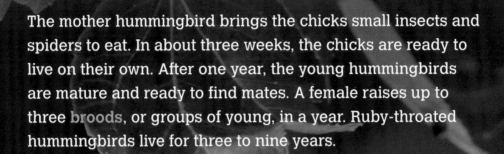

A mother hummingbird watches over her chicks and nest for about three weeks.

RUBY-THROATED HUMMINGBIRDS VS. PAINTED BUNTINGS

In a sunny field, a male painted bunting hops and flutters his wings. He is courting a female, who is pecking the ground nearby. Painted buntings live in woods, fields, and thickets in Central America and the southeastern United States. They share similar life cycles with ruby-throated hummingbirds.

After the male and female painted bunting mate, the female builds a nest in a tree and lays three to four eggs. About twelve days later, the eggs hatch. Like ruby-throated hummingbirds, the young painted buntings are tiny and nearly bare of feathers. Their mother brings them insects to eat. When the chicks are about a month old, they can feed themselves.

The colors of the female painted bunting help camouflage her in the nest.

Male painted buntings sometimes help feed their young. Female painted buntings raise up to two broods in a year. Like ruby-throated hummingbirds, painted buntings are mature and ready to mate when they are one year old. They usually live between five and ten years.

RUBY-THROATED HUMMINGBIRDS VS. RED-NECKED PHALAROPES

On the marshy shore of a pond, a male red-necked phalarope sits in a nest. Red-necked phalaropes breed in wetlands across the Arctic tundra. Their life cycles are different from the life cycles of ruby-throated hummingbirds.

Male ruby-throated hummingbirds chase away other males, while females raise the chicks. For red-necked phalaropes, those roles are switched. Female phalaropes court males and chase away other females. Males raise the chicks.

After mating, the female red-necked phalarope lays three or four eggs in a nest on the ground. The female leaves after laying the eggs. The male sits on them for about three weeks until they hatch. Red-necked phalarope chicks are born covered with fluffy down and can walk and feed themselves shortly after hatching. Red-necked phalaropes are mature and ready to mate in one year. They live up to five years.

A red-necked phalarope stretches its wings on the shore of a pond.

COMPARE IT!

RUBY-THROATED HUMMINGBIRDS

VS.

RED-NECKED PHALAROPES

1 TO 3 ◀ NUMBER OF EGGS ▶ **3 TO 4**

Mother ◀ MAIN CAREGIVER ▶ Father

3 TO 9 YEARS ◀ LIFE SPAN ▶ **UP TO 5 YEARS**

RUBY-THROATED HUMMINGBIRD TRAIT CHART

This book explores ruby-throated hummingbirds and the ways they are similar to and different from other birds. What other birds would you like to learn about?

	FEATHERS ON BODY	WARM-BLOODED	LAYS HARD-SHELLED EGGS	DRINKS NECTAR	ACROBATIC FLIER	MIGRATES
RUBY-THROATED HUMMINGBIRD	X	X	X	X	X	X
ANNA'S HUMMINGBIRD	X	X	X	X	X	X
AUSTRALIAN PELICAN	X	X	X			X
ORCHARD ORIOLE	X	X	X	X		X
ADÉLIE PENGUIN	X	X	X			X
RUFOUS HUMMINGBIRD	X	X	X	X	X	X
TURKEY VULTURE	X	X	X			X
PAINTED BUNTING	X	X	X			X
RED-NECKED PHALAROPE	X	X	X			X

GLOSSARY

beaks: the jaws and mouths of birds. Beaks are sometimes called bills, especially when they are long and flat.

breed: to produce offspring

broods: groups of young that are hatched or cared for at one time

camouflage: to hide or disguise something by covering it up or changing the way it looks

carnivores: meat-eating animals

carrion: dead and decaying flesh

down: a covering of soft, fluffy feathers

habitats: environments where an animal lives. A habitat is the place where an animal can find food, water, air, shelter, and a place to raise its young.

incubates: keeps eggs warm and under good conditions before they hatch

migrate: to pass from one place to another on a regular schedule for feeding or raising young

nectar: a sugary liquid in plants that attracts birds for pollination

omnivores: animals that eat both meat and plants

territory: an area that is occupied and defended by an animal or group of animals

traits: features that are inherited from parents. Body size and skin color are examples of inherited traits.

tundra: a cold, treeless Arctic plain that has a permanently frozen layer below the ground's surface

warm-blooded: able to maintain a constant body temperature independent of the surroundings

LERNER

SOURCE

Expand learning beyond the printed book. Download free, complementary educational resources for this book from our website, www.lernerresource.com.

SELECTED BIBLIOGRAPHY

"All about Birds." Cornell Lab of Ornithology. Accessed March 28, 2015. http://www.allaboutbirds.org/guide/.

"Animals." *National Geographic*. Accessed March 28, 2015. http://animals .nationalgeographic.com/animals/.

Birds of North America Online. Cornell Lab of Ornithology. Accessed March 28, 2015. http://bna.birds.cornell.edu/bna.

Chambers, Lanny. "Ruby-Throated Hummingbird." Hummingbirds.net. Accessed April 7, 2015. http://www .hummingbirds.net/rubythroated.html.

Vuilleumier, Francois, and the American Museum of Natural History. *Birds of North America*. New York: DK, 2009.

FURTHER INFORMATION

Alderfer, Jonathan K. *National Geographic Kids Bird Guide of North America: The Best Birding Book for Kids from National Geographic's Bird Experts*. Washington, DC: National Geographic, 2013. This book will show you how to identify ruby-throated hummingbirds and more than one hundred other species of North American birds. You'll learn fun facts about each bird's life cycle.

Johnson, Jinny. *Animal Planet™ Wild World: An Encyclopedia of Animals*. Minneapolis: Millbrook Press, 2012. In this Animal Planet™ encyclopedia, you'll learn more about hummingbirds and many of the world's other fascinating animals.

Journey North: Hummingbird Facts
http://www.learner.org/jnorth/search /Hummer.html
Check out this site for answers to your questions about hummingbirds from hummingbird expert Lanny Chambers.

Smithsonian Migratory Bird Center: Hummingbirds
https://nationalzoo.si.edu/scbi /migratorybirds/webcam/hummingbirds .cfm
Discover different kinds of hummingbirds as well as facts, photos, and suggestions for how you can help these tiny creatures.

INDEX